Fact Finders®

Amazing Animal Colonies

CORALS
Secrets of Their Reef-Making Colonies

by Rebecca Stefoff

Consultant:
Robert S. Steneck, PhD
Professor of Oceanography, Marine Biology and Policy
School of Marine Sciences
University of Maine

D1716939

CAPSTONE PRESS
a capstone imprint

Fact Finders Books are published by Capstone Press,
1710 Roe Crest Drive, North Mankato, Minnesota 56003
www.mycapstone.com

Library of Congress Cataloging-in-Publication Data
Names: Stefoff, Rebecca, 1951- author.
Title: Corals : secrets of their reef-making colonies / by Rebecca Stefoff.
Description: North Mankato, Minnesota : An imprint of Capstone Press, [2019]
   | Series: Fact Finders. Amazing animal colonies | Audience: Ages: 8-9. |
Identifiers: LCCN 2018029019 (print) | LCCN 2018032451 (ebook) | ISBN
   9781543555608 (eBook PDF) | ISBN 9781543555561 (hardcover) | ISBN
   9781543559132 (paperback)
Subjects: LCSH: Corals—Juvenile literature.
Classification: LCC QL377.C5 (ebook) | LCC QL377.C5 S74 2019 (print) | DDC
   593.6—dc23
LC record available at https://lccn.loc.gov/2018029019

Editorial Credits
Editor: Carrie Braulick Sheely
Designer: Ted Williams
Media Researcher: Heather Mauldin
Production specialist: Katy LaVigne

Photo Credits
Ardea Picture Library: Miles Kelly Publishing, 15; Getty Images: Ann Ronan Pictures/Print Collector, 7, Auscape/UIG, 22 (bottom), Wild Horizons/UIG, 19; iStockphoto: Eloi_Omella, 9, johnandersonphoto, 10 (top right), xantuanx, 10 (bottom left); Shutterstock: aquapix, cover (background), Ethan Daniels, 25, ifish, 14, John A. Anderson, cover (top), Jolanta Wojcicka, cover (bottom), 1, kaschibo, 11, Konstantin Novikov, 17, Rich Carey, 4, Richard Whitcombe, 29, superjoseph, 22 (middle), Tanya Puntti, 22 (top), Tara Melinda, 8, think4photop, 26, timsimages, 23, Tyler Fox, 13

Printed and bound in the USA.
PA48

Table of Contents

MANY INTO ONE

Imagine yourself scuba diving in a warm ocean. You breathe air from a tank on your back. Gently moving your feet, you glide forward. In front of you, a ridge rises from the sandy bottom. It is a coral reef. You look across the reef. You see wrinkled lumps like brains and branches like deer antlers.

Corals of a reef can be one of several shapes.

The reef is full of life. A crab walks across it. An octopus slips into a hole. Brightly colored fish swim nearby. The reef looks solid and it stays in place. But the reef itself is alive too!

A coral reef is made up of corals. Each coral is made up of large numbers of individual animals called **polyps**. The polyps' small bodies look like flowers. They are soft and boneless. Polyps build their own skeletons outside their soft bodies. A reef may look like it is made of stone or cement. It is really made of skeletons of millions of polyps.

The Colonies of a Coral Reef

As the polyps multiply, they stick together in growths or groups called **colonies**. A reef is a cluster or string of colonies that are close together.

Many different kinds of corals exist. They live in a wide variety of places in the oceans. Only some of them build reefs.

polyp—a small sea animal with a tubular body and a round mouth surrounded by tentacles

colony—a large group of animals of the same species that live together

CHAPTER TWO

SOLVING THE MYSTERIES OF CORAL

It took scientists a long time to figure out just what corals are and how they live. People began studying the natural world thousands of years ago. One of the first steps for early scientists was to sort what they found into groups. Plants were one group. Animals were another group.

Coral was a problem for these early scientists. They could not decide if it was a plant, an animal, or a form of life that was neither plant nor animal. Some scientists even thought it was a **mineral**.

Seeing the Invisible World

In the 1000s a Middle Eastern scientist named Al-Biruni said that coral is an animal. He was right. But for another 700 years people in Europe believed that coral was a plant.

William Herschel was a German musician and scientist. After moving to England in 1757, he discovered the planet Uranus.

Herschel also experimented with microscopes. These tools let people see things too small to be seen by the human eye. Herschel studied coral polyps under a microscope. He saw that the **cells** of a polyp have thin walls like an animal's. Plant cells have thick walls. Herschel knew that coral was an animal.

mineral—a substance found in nature that is not made by a plant or animal

cell—a basic part of an animal or plant that is so small you can't see it without a microscope

↑William Herschel mainly studied space, but he also studied living things, such as coral.

Ancient Corals

The very first corals appeared long before fish or land plants lived. Ancient corals built reefs that are now **fossil** remains around the world. The oldest known fossil corals are more than 500 million years old.

One ancient fossil reef is on Manitoulin Island, Canada. It formed about 425 million years ago. At the time, this part of Canada was very hot. A warm, shallow ocean covered the area. People have found fossils of many coral colonies there.

The oldest corals were not closely related to modern corals. All of the ancient coral **species** died out over time. Modern corals began to appear around 230 million years ago. At that time, dinosaurs lived on Earth.

an ancient coral fossil from about 400 million years ago

Some types of coral look like fans.

Today's Corals

More than 6,000 species of corals now live in the world's oceans. Most of them are found in warm, shallow waters in or close to the **tropics**. Other corals live in cold, deep parts of the sea.

Corals belong to a large group of animals without backbones called cnidarians. Most cnidarians live in the sea, but a few types live in lakes or streams. Jellyfish are also cnidarians. Jellyfish drift or swim through the water. But corals are fixed in place. They never move.

fossil—the remains or traces of plants and animals that are preserved as rock

species—a group of closely related organisms that can produce offspring

tropics—a warm region of Earth that is near the equator

9

Hexacorals and Octocorals

Corals fall into two groups. One group's members are called the hexacorals. They have six **tentacles** or multiples of six tentacles. The stony corals that build reefs are hexacorals.

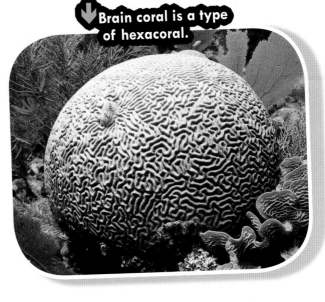

Brain coral is a type of hexacoral.

Members of the second group are called octocorals. They have eight tentacles or multiples of eight tentacles. Most octocorals are soft corals. They do not make skeletons around their polyps nor build reefs. However, some octocorals make a hard skeleton under their polyps.

Gorgonians are a type of octocoral.

tentacle—a long, flexible limb used for moving, feeling, and grabbing

10

BEWARE OF FIRE!

Don't be fooled by the name "fire coral." Only half of it is true. Fire corals are not true corals. Like true corals, fire corals are cnidarians. But they are not closely related to real corals. About 15 species of fire corals exist. They live in colonies of polyps with hard outer skeletons. Fire corals often grow on reefs in tropical waters. Their colonies are yellowish-green or brown. In shape they often look like branching plants. The "fire" part of the name comes from the pain they can cause. Swimmers or divers often mistake fire coral for seaweed. They touch it or brush against it. The polyps then sting. The pain usually lasts a few days. To avoid being stung, always be careful not to touch or brush against anything on a reef. This protects the reef life too.

CHAPTER THREE

THE LIFE OF A POLYP

Coral polyps are simple animals. They have few parts. Yet each part does an important job. A coral colony depends on the survival of the individual polyps in it.

A Close-Up Look

A coral polyp is mostly a stomach shaped like a bag. At the top is a mouth surrounded by tentacles. The tentacles move food into the mouth and waste out of it. Polyps stretch out their tentacles to search for food.

AMAZING FACT

Coral polyps vary in size from .25 inch (0.6 centimeter) to 12 inches (30 cm) long. Most are smaller than 1 inch (2.5 cm).

The polyp's stomach is divided into vertical sections called mesenteries. The mesenteries digest the polyp's food. At the bottom of the mesenteries are long tubes called filaments. If a polyp is under stress, it can shoot these filaments out of its mouth. Corals sometimes use the filaments to fight with other corals or animals.

the mouth of a plate coral

Each stony polyp sits in an outer skeleton called a corallite. This outer skeleton is made of a stony or bony mineral called calcium carbonate. Polyps create calcium carbonate. It leaves their bodies through tiny openings in their bases. The mineral hardens and builds up around them to form the corallites. All stony corals can pull in their tentacles to disappear into their corallites.

In every stony coral colony, a thin layer of living tissue lies on top of the calcium carbonate. It links the polyps together into one giant organism. Through this tissue the polyps share nutrients. They grow at the same speed. They do not have to compete with one another for food. Whether stony or soft, polyps never move around.

Honeycomb coral corallites form low cone shapes.

A CORAL POLYP

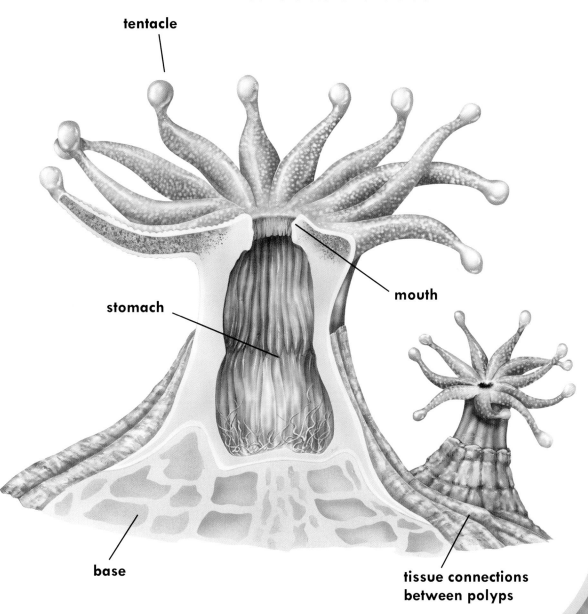

tentacle

mouth

stomach

base

tissue connections
between polyps

How Corals Eat

Corals eat in two ways. One way is by using their tentacles to catch **prey** that comes within reach. Small polyps feed on tiny drifting sea creatures called plankton and other small animals. Larger polyps may catch small fish.

Polyps have soft bodies, but they still pack a powerful punch. Their tentacles have cells called nematocysts. These stingers are loaded with **venom**. When the tentacles brush against prey, the nematocysts sting it. The tentacles pull the animal through the polyp's mouth into its stomach.

Some stony corals also get nutrients from the inside. In shallow water reached by sunlight, coral polyps have tiny **algae** called zooxanthellae living inside them. The zooxanthellae and the polyps have a partnership. Each species helps the other. The zooxanthellae gain a safe home and a source of food. They live by eating some of the polyp's waste products. Like green plants on land, zooxanthellae contain a chemical called chlorophyll. It turns sunlight into sugars and other nutrients that the polyps use for energy. This process is called photosynthesis.

prey—an animal hunted by another animal for food

venom—a poisonous liquid produced by some animals

algae—small plants without roots or stems that grow in water

Tentacles are packed with nematocysts.

AMAZING FACT

The bodies of stony polyps are clear. The zooxanthellae give the corals their color.

Making More Polyps

Corals reproduce in several ways. Some colonies create new polyps in more than one way. Some corals are brooders. Their eggs grow inside the coral. Oval-shaped **larvae** come out of the eggs.

Corals also may release reproductive cells called sperm and eggs into the water. This process is called spawning. The corals in a colony spawn at the same time. When a sperm and egg join, they form an embryo. It becomes a larva.

Larvae float on the water's surface. Animals eat many of the larvae. After a few days or weeks, the survivors sink to the bottom. They settle into the sand. The larvae turn into polyps, and new colonies begin.

Adult Copies

Adult polyps make **identical** copies of themselves. They bud or split to make these copies. In budding a smaller polyp sprouts from an adult. As its body forms, it separates from the adult. But they remain connected by living tissue. In splitting adult polyps split in half. Each half then grows the body parts it needs.

MASS SPAWNING AFTER A FULL MOON

Some stony corals take part in a mating event called mass spawning. Colonies and whole reefs release all of their reproductive cells into the water over several days or weeks. Clouds of tiny sperm and eggs swirl through the water. Egg and sperm cells live for only a few hours. Mass spawning gives them the best chance to pair up. But how do corals know when to release their reproductive cells? Mass spawning happens at night. Often it is right after a full moon. Scientists think that polyps have cells that can sense light and temperature. A combination of moonlight, water temperature, and even the tides might tell the corals when to spawn.

boulder star coral during mass spawn

larva—a coral polyp at the stage of development between an egg and an adult

identical—exactly alike

CHAPTER FOUR

BUILDING COLONIES AND REEFS

Coral reefs have been called "the rain forests of the sea." Rain forests on land have a big variety of plant and animal life. At sea, reefs are also rich **habitats**. One-quarter of all sea species live in, on, or near coral reefs.

How and Where Reefs Grow

A reef starts when the polyp skeletons in a colony start to make a structure. Sometimes one adult polyp leaves a colony, drifts a short distance away, and starts a new colony. A storm or other disturbance also might break a colony into pieces. These new colonies are separate but identical, like twins.

Most reef-building corals live above a depth of about 150 feet (46 meters). Some polyps need light to grow quickly. These corals usually live above a depth of 60 feet (18 m).

habitat—the natural place and conditions in which an animal or plant lives

The water temperature also must meet the needs of reef-building corals. Many types live in water that is between 64 degrees Fahrenheit (18 degrees Celsius) and 85°F (29°C). Several dozen species live in hotter waters in the Persian Gulf. Other species live in deep, cold water, such as areas off the coast of Norway and Canada. Deep-water polyps grow close together in mounds or "forests." But they don't build reefs that reach the surface.

The World's Coral Reefs

coral reef location

Types of Reefs

Coral reefs come in many shapes. Here are the four most common shapes:

Fringing reefs are attached to land or are very close to land. Either no water or only a narrow shallow channel of water lies between them and the shore.

Barrier reefs are farther from the shore than fringing reefs. The channel between a barrier reef and the shore may be deep or shallow.

Platform reefs often lie between fringing and barrier reefs. They form on top of mountains or ridges that rise from the sea floor to near the surface.

Atoll reefs are ring-shaped with shallow pools of water called lagoons in the center. Built-up sand can turn an atoll reef into a circle of flat islands.

HUMAN-MADE REEFS

Sometimes people make artificial reefs. People create these reefs to protect beaches from storms and to replace damaged natural reefs. Most of them are planned mainly to be habitats for corals and other reef life.

People can make artificial reefs out of different materials. Governments sink old or damaged ships, subway cars, and other large objects in places where corals can live. Algae and coral polyps attach themselves to the sunken objects. Soon a reef begins to form. Artists have also created underwater sculptures that become home to algae, corals, and other sea life.

Many artificial reefs have become healthy marine environments. But a few have leaked chemicals into the ocean. Some have drawn so many visitors that natural reefs nearby are damaged by too much use. Artificial reefs can be good for the ocean, but only if they are carefully planned and built.

CHAPTER FIVE

AN UNKNOWN FUTURE

Many animals, plants, and their habitats face challenges today. This is true of corals and coral reefs. Human actions threaten them. Changes in the oceans do too. But many scientists think that we can help corals survive.

Threats to Reefs

Some threats to reefs are local. People damage coral reefs in many ways. They mine coral to use as building blocks for roads or houses. They blow up reefs to stun fish and make them easy to catch. They pollute coastal waters with waste and chemicals.

Other threats are widespread. Ocean temperatures are slowly rising. These high temperatures are causing stress for corals. When corals are stressed, stony polyps lose their zooxanthellae. The color that the algae give them fades away. Only the skeleton can be seen through the polyps' bodies. Scientists call this problem coral bleaching.

Bleached coral looks white because it has lost its zooxanthellae.

Corals that are too stressed may not recover. Once the polyps are dead, animals such as sponges and worms move into the dead coral. They dig holes that weaken the reef. Over time, the reef can crumble and fall apart. The variety of life that it supported will disappear.

High sea temperatures in 2016 and 2017 brought coral bleaching to Australia's Great Barrier Reef. It killed half the coral in the northern part of the reef. Coral also died in the central section. The loss of coral means that there may not be enough new larvae to rebuild the lost reef sections.

When a coral reef dies, it no longer supports a variety of marine life.

Another threat to corals is a change in the chemical makeup of ocean water. People use fossil fuels such as oil and coal to produce energy. The use of these fuels releases carbon dioxide into the air. Some of it enters the oceans. Carbon dioxide then increases the acidity of the water. This change is called acidification. It keeps corals from absorbing the calcium carbonate they need to maintain their skeletons. Their skeletons will then dissolve and the coral reef will break down.

THE GREAT BARRIER REEF

A chain of more than 3,000 reefs and 1,000 islands runs for more than 1,400 miles (2,550 kilometers) near Australia's northeastern coast. It is Earth's largest living structure. This is the Great Barrier Reef.

The Great Barrier Reef is home to about 400 types of corals and more than 1,500 species of fish. Each year more than 2 million visitors dive, swim, or boat near the reef. The reef is worth $3.7 to $4.5 billion a year to Australia.

AMAZING FACT
People in space can see the Great Barrier Reef.

Protecting the World's Corals

Many people are working to protect coral reefs. Scientists and members of the tourist industry work with local communities to end the mining and blowing up of reefs. They teach people how to avoid polluting coastal areas. They show how healthy reefs can attract fish. Fishing opportunities can then attract tourists who spend money in the area. Other groups are helping people start businesses, such as diving tours, that use reefs without harming them.

Overfishing happens when too many fish are taken out of an area. The fish cannot replace themselves. Around the Great Barrier Reef, overfishing has cut the number of fish that eat the crown-of-thorns starfish. This starfish eats the polyps of stony corals. Crown-of-thorns starfish are killing corals in the Great Barrier Reef and other places. To protect the corals, special teams of divers kill starfish by the thousands. Other efforts are aimed at ending overfishing.

Rising water temperature and acidification are problems too big for one community or government to solve. Some people are using cleaner energy sources instead of fossil fuels. These sources include wind energy and solar power. Working together, people can help make sure that corals and their reefs will survive for years into the future.

A crown-of-thorns starfish feeds on bleached coral.

Glossary

algae (AL-jee)—small plants without roots or stems that grow in water

cell (SEL)—a basic part of an animal or plant that is so small you can't see it without a microscope

colony (KAH-luh-nee)—a large group of animals of the same species that live together

fossil (FAH-suhl)—the remains or traces of an animal or plant, preserved as rock

habitat (HAB-uh-tat)—the natural place and conditions in which an animal or plant lives

identical (eye-DEN-ti-kuhl)—exactly alike

larva (LAR-vuh)—a coral polyp at the stage of development between an egg and an adult

mineral (MIN-ur-uhl)—a substance found in nature that is not made by a plant or animal

polyp (PAH-lup)—a small sea animal with a tubular body and a round mouth surrounded by tentacles

prey (PRAY)—an animal hunted by another animal for food

species (SPEE-sheez)—a group of closely related organisms that can produce offspring

tentacle (TEN-tuh-kuhl)—a long, flexible limb used for moving, feeling, and grabbing

tropics (TRAH-piks)—a warm region of Earth that is near the equator

venom (VEN-uhm)—a poisonous liquid produced by some animals

Read More

Fiedler, Heidi. *Coral: A Close-Up Photographic Look Inside Your World.* Lake Forest, Cal.: The Quatro Group, 2017.

Messner, Kate. *The Brilliant Deep: Rebuilding the World's Coral Reefs.* San Francisco: Chronicle Books, 2018.

Critical Thinking Questions

1. Why are corals considered "rain forests of the sea?" What other living things interact with them, and how? Use online or other sources to support your answer.
2. Corals and zooxanthellae have a relationship in which one organism helps the other. This relationship is called mutualism. Can you think of other animals that have this type of relationship? Use online or other sources to support your answer.
3. Which type of effort to help protect corals do you think will be most effective? Why?

Internet Sites

Use FactHound to find Internet sites related to this book.
Visit *www.facthound.com*
Just type in 9781543555561 and go.

 Check out projects, games and lots more at
www.capstonekids.com

Index